Time Well Spent

a journal from the author of

Horse, Follow Closely

GaWaNi Pony Boy

photographs by Gabrielle Boiselle

A DIVISION OF FANCY PUBLICATIONS
Irvine, California

Ruth Berman, editor-in-chief
Nick Clemente, special consultant
Cover and book design copyright © 1999 by Michele Lanci-Altomare. All rights reserved.

Text and photos adapted from *Horse, Follow Closely.*
Text copyright © 1998 by GaWaNi Pony Boy
Photographs copyright © 1998 by Gabrielle Boiselle

The horses in this journal are referred to as either *he* or *she*.

Library of Congress Catalog Card Number: 98-74810
ISBN: 1-889540-42-0

BowTie™ Press
A Division of Fancy Publications
3 Burroughs
Irvine, California 92618

Manufactured in the United States of America
10 9 8 7 6 5 4 3 2 1

To the Creator, the Elders,
and the Veterans

—GaWaNi PonyBoy

Introduction

I FORGET THAT TIME IS A HUMAN INVENTION.
We often hear the phrase *before time*. It would be just as accurate to say, *before humans felt the need to quantify, to become more efficient, to maximize profits, to duplicate their efforts and move away from instinct.* Have you ever said, *I'm hungry*, only to follow that statement with *what time is it?* We have become so dependent on time that when our bodies tell us that we are hungry, we must first consult the watch on our wrist or the clock on the wall to verify that our bodies' messages are indeed sincere. *It's six o'clock, I should eat something!*

Too often I'm reminded not of the importance of time but rather of the urgency that time has in my life. Horses remind me of this.

What is time to a horse? Sure there's feeding time and there is nap time, but beyond these things, what is time to a horse? There is no prescribed time in which a new foal must learn to run from a predator. Foals know only that they must learn to run before being eaten. There are no certain number of hours that a prospective alpha horse must spend proving herself capable of that position.

So what is time to a horse? Time is survival. Time is relationship. Time is herd status. Time is family.

I am dumbfounded but not surprised by the individual who asks me, *Why is it important to spend a day with your horse?* Beyond the obvious benefits that this form of meditation can provide, there are more practical reasons.

To a horse, relationship is everything. Every move a horse makes is determined by the relationship that exists between her and the other members of her herd.

Her herd is her life—entirely. If you or I aspire to become the leader of a herd (which we all need to do if we wish to enjoy the company of our horses), we must cultivate that relationship, not just happen upon it. Before we can develop a relationship with a horse, we must first get acquainted with the individual. We must spend time getting to know *who* rather than *what* the horse is. There have been hundreds of books devoted to the subject of *what* the horse is, but only through passive observation can we discover *who* horses are. Horses are intelligent, and horses are unique individuals.

Some of my proudest moments are when an enthused person approaches me with comments something like, *You know, you could never have convinced me of the benefits my horse and I would receive from this exercise. I learned who my horse is.* The intriguing part of spending time with your horse is that the answers come before the questions are asked. You will find yourself saying things such as, *Oh that is why he does that* or *I never knew that would motivate her.*

When teaching horses, there are only two instances of time that you need to be concerned with. They are 1) *Teacher, I don't understand,* and 2) *I understand now.* Beyond these two "times" there are no hours or minutes. The horse does not understand that an hour and five minutes has past. She only understands that her teacher has not yet comforted her by saying, *Thank you...well done.* When teaching horses, forget time. The concept of time does not exist in the mind of your student. Therefore, it does not exist.

The horse is a magnificent part of Creation that I will never fully understand. Her patience is endless, her intelligence wondrous. Yet she has no need for time. She has only family. I think that our understanding of family is one of the few comparisons that we can make to the mind of the horse. The concept of family is a window to a world without time. In a family, time has no meaning. There is relationship, there is status, love, joy, sorrow, but other than respect for the Elders and understanding for the young, time does not have a hold on our understanding of family.

To be accepted as family by our equine companions is the highest honor that we can receive from them. To be chosen as alpha, to be entrusted with their safety, and to be charged with their education are not things that we should take lightly. To be fully capable of these things we must, above all else, spend what we call time with our horses.

How does your horse react
     when he first notices
you're around?

Does your horse enjoy being touched or petted in certain areas of his body?

Are there areas of your horse's body that he protects or avoids having touched?

Visions

What is your horse's reaction to people who
            come up to the fence or enter the pasture,
to horses on the other side of the fence,
                        or to other species?

Does your horse approach others in his environment?
Does he approach them in a friendly way?
In a territorial way? Does he ignore them?
If so, for how long? _____

_____

_____

_____

_____

_____

_____

_____

_____

_____

_____

_____

_____

_____

_____

_____

_____

_____

_____

_____

_____

_____

Verse

When developing a relationship with your horse, there is no substitute for spending time together.

TIME WELL SPENT WITH YOUR HORSE
means much more than
performing daily tasks in his presence.
It means time spent observing him;
it means unencumbered time spent
living near him, for there are
many things about your horse
that you don't and can't know
unless you spend time together.

Does your horse enjoy the company of other species, including dogs, cats, and even birds?

When another person removes a horse from
the pasture, does your horse tag along?
Harass the horse who is being led?
Pester the person for treats or attention?

Visions

Observe your horse both indoors and outdoors:
Do her eyes run when she's either inside or outside?
Does her nose run?
Does the consistency of her manure change?

How many times a day does your horse roll?
Where and how does she roll? Does she roll only
when other horses are away from her?

Verse

If we can understand what it means to be a horse, react like a horse, and relate to other things like a horse, then we can have a more productive relationship with a horse.

NATIVE AMERICANS
did not attempt
to treat the horse
as they would a dog
or a human but instead
trained, rode, and
communicated within
the boundaries set forth
by the nature of the horse.

*Observe how your horse interacts
with his herd members.
Can you tell who your horse likes best?*

Are there any members of the herd
who irritate your horse?
How does he handle them—does he get in squabbles
or does he normally back down?

Visions

Does your horse initiate physical contact
with his herdmates? Is it Positive? Negative?

Is your horse patient with the intrusive behavior of his herdmates?

Verse

Horses are individuals,
and unless we understand
the individual we cannot
expect the individual
to understand us.

W HEN I WANTED TO
learn how to
communicate with
my horse, I learned
that the best place
to start is by
consulting my horse,
not by asking
a two-legged.

How does your horse respond to a herd member's request for mutual grooming or fly-swatting?

Does your horse stay with the herd or does she venture off by herself (or with a friend)?

Visions

Does your horse vocalize more or less than her herdmates?

When and why does your horse vocalize?

Verse

To secure a true partnering relationship and forge open communication with your horse, very specific tools are needed, the most important of which is time.

Your time together is not just
time when you happen to be
in the same space. Hand grazing,
taking a walk, grooming
(for no purpose other than to
connect with your horse),
and hanging out in the pasture
are all opportunities to deepen
the relationship with your horse.

Does your horse initiate a herd gallop?
Does he watch as herdmates
get a good gallop going
or does he participate?

Compared to his pasturemates, how sensitive is your horse to his surroundings? Does he swivel his ears, stop grazing to look around, and continue to look at disturbances long after the rest of the horses have returned to grazing?

Visions

*Is your horse a picky eater,
choosing grass from each section
of the pasture, or does he
"sweep" an entire area?*

How much water does your horse drink?

Verse

Walk in front

of your horse

expecting him to follow,

and he will.

THE FIRST SET OF STAIRS I ENCOUNTERED
with Kola was treated no differently
than a grassy hill. I held his lead,
did not change my pace, did not
look back to see if he could make it,
and simply walked up.
Kola climbs steps and rides in elevators
because I never gave him any reason
to believe that he couldn't.

Does your horse play in the water trough,
chew on tree branches or fence boards,
paw the dirt, shake her head a lot,
or scratch herself on fence posts?

Where is your horse's favorite place to nap?

Visions

*Where on your horse's body
does she sweat the most?*

Does your horse have a favorite bathroom area?
If so, why does she prefer
that location?

Verse

Simple yet rewarding, spending a day with a horse is an important exercise. It requires no special talents or skills, but the rider gets dramatic results.

W<small>HEN YOU ARE THE</small> *ITANCAN,*

or leader, of your herd,

your horse will always look to you

for guidance and direction.

You must not only give the animal a

reason to feel secure but you must

always maintain the status as

the leader of the herd—

a herd of two, rider and horse.

Do your horse's moods change depending on the time of day?

GaWaNi Pony Boy is mixed blood Tsa-la-gi, full blood human. After attending college in Boston, MA, he spent three years traveling the United States with a Native American drum group. It was during these on-the-road years that he was able to seek the advice and council of Tribal Elders from many different Nations and backgrounds to learn about the beliefs and methods used by this Nation's first great horsemen. By weaving the "old ways" with his own already successful training methods, Pony has developed Relationship Training. When not writing, GaWaNi Pony Boy can be found presenting clinics and seminars in an effort to help people get more enjoyment from the companionship of their horses and have a better understanding of our relationship with all things.

Gabrielle Boiselle is a well-known international horse photographer. Her understanding, patience, and intuition create special images that capture the soul and emotion of her subjects. Born of a horse breeder family, she decided to become a journalist and studied science of communication in Munich, Germany. Upon finishing her studies, she worked in broadcasting and on TV in Germany and traveled through Asia and the Arabian countries working for European magazines. Gabrielle Boiselle has traveled around the world photographing horses and creating calendars and books. She lives in Speyer, Germany.

Other Books by GaWaNi Pony Boy:
Horse, Follow Closely
Out of the Saddle

For more information about GaWaNi Pony Boy or to find out about our other horse titles, visit our Web site at
www.animalnetwork.com

To know when Pony will be giving a clinic in your area, visit his Web site at
www.horsenet.com/ponyboy